Joan's Story

First edition published 2020

Joan Dudman is the author of this work
Cover illustration by Joan Dudman
Edited by Claire Bower
Published by Claire Bower 2020

Copyright Joan Dudman
All Rights Reserved

No part of this publication may be reproduced, distributed, or transmitted in any form or by any means, including photocopying, recording, or other electronic or mechanical methods, without the prior written permission of the publisher, except in the case of noncommercial uses permitted by copyright law. For permission requests, write to the publisher, addressed "Attention: Permissions Coordinator," at the address below.

5 The Vale, Skelton, York. YO30 1YH

Ordering Information:
Quantity sales. Special discounts are available on quantity purchases at Lulu.com

Available at Amazon.co.uk

ISBN 978-0-244-87581-7

Dedication

Thank you Lord Jesus, for all you have done in my life. You are so good to me!

Joan's Story

Introduction

It is the day after Christmas 2007 and I am laid in bed with a horrid chest infection. All the family had a lovely time at our Julie's (my eldest daughter's) on Boxing Day. Julie and her husband, John, made a wonderful curry and all the trimmings. Thoughtfully, they sent me some home, bless them.

We are a large family and almost everyone went to Julie's 'do'.

We have five children; four girls and one boy. Good kids, as my husband always refers to them. We are grandparents now, too. There are fourteen, from Daisy, aged two, to Nathan, aged eighteen. Grandad counted 23 at Julie's, quite a handful! It was a pity I missed it because they all had a lovely time, laughing and joking and eating and drinking. I am so glad for them all.

Last night I felt so ill. I thought, 'What if I die?' My mind drifted back along the years; it has passed so quickly. We have been so well blessed with such a lovely family. We have had our share of problems, with one or two, but, with God's help we have overcome.

As a young woman, I would have fought off this chest infection and even carried on working, but, now, in my late 60s it has knocked me for six. Never mind, it is time to remember the lovely things that happened after my divorce...

Chapter 1

It was 1976, my marriage had broken down and I was on my own with three daughters to care for. I thought, 'How can there be a god?' How could he let this nightmare, that I had been through happen to me? I felt so alone.

The days passed into weeks. I was so desperately lonely. I got on my knees in the lounge and looked up at the ceiling and said, 'If there is a god above this ceiling, help me!'

Well, believe it or not, sort of miracles started to happen. I was desperate for somewhere to live. I had my name down for a council house, but the waiting list was around ten years, at that time. Well, I got one in seven months! I was over the moon. So, then I asked again, 'Please God, send me a good kind family man, like St. Joseph, to look after me and mine.

I hardly ever went out, but I was asked on a nurse's leaving do, so I went. We went to 71 Club, on Micklegate. I wasn't enjoying it very much so I decided to go home because they all seemed like silly kids. I was 36. I said my goodbyes and walked across the dance floor when someone tapped me on the shoulder and asked me to dance. I turned around and looked into the eyes of a lovely looking chap of similar age to me. My heart flipped. I thought, 'He's nice.' We danced and danced 'til everyone had left. Then he took me to the taxi and asked to see me again.

We just clicked. It was wonderful and I was on cloud nine. His name was Bob.

Chapter 2

I saw Bob again and again. What a time I had. Bob took me dancing and bought me flowers. He was a lovely dancer and used to swing me around and sing to me. We were always laughing. We were really happy.

After years of unhappiness and fear and dark days, I had broken through into happiness; sheer joy.

If I was called to the phone at work I knew it would be Bob. I was so excited and giddy. My old neighbour, Mr. Johnson said, 'He is always on time. I watch him picking you up. He will be reliable.'

My daughters were happy for me too, because I was happy. The fearful days were a thing of the past.

Bob had been divorced for seven years and was looking after his two children with the help of an old chap. Bob had a good job and worked long hour shift work. He was dark around his eyes with tiredness doing nights. He always bucked up when he met me.

The time came when I could move into my new home and, low and behold, it was only a mile away from Bob's home. We were able to see each other every day. Bob said, 'I must see you every day, even if it is only for five minutes.'
Bless him.

I hired a removal van with my last £40 and we all piled on; the girls and me. Off we went, waving happily to the lovely neighbours, who were wishing us well.

We were all excited. The new house was lovely. It was decorated throughout, although it had no carpets. It didn't matter, so I put the old ones down. We were so happy. The girls changed schools and they were happy. Julie's boyfriend, Martin, came knocking at the door, so she was happy too.

I was on a bus route for work at the hospital and there were local shops at hand. Walking back from the shops I said, 'Thank you' to God and I said the Lord's Prayer, that we used to say at school. I was carrying my shopping in my arms, as it was heavy. When I got to the bit in the Lord's Prayer where it says: 'Give us this day our daily bread', a bite sized lump of bread fell onto my shopping. I laughed out loud and thought, 'God has a sense of humour! or has a bird dropped some bread? Which one?'

Chapter 3

That summer Bob went to Somerset for a two week holiday with his children, Jenny and Andrew. It was then that I realised how very much I thought of him. I missed him terribly. We talked on the phone, (using the old phone box in the street). Bob wrote me some lovely love letters, which I still keep. Those two weeks seemed an age.

On his return, Bob took me out for a drink. He put a little box on the table before me. The he disappeared to the men's room. I opened the box, and there, to my delight, was an engagement ring. It was lovely. I tried it on and it fitted perfectly.

We had a little engagement party at my house. Andrew, who was only nine, said, 'Raise your glasses everyone, to Job and Bo!' Everyone laughed as he muddled his words. It was a lovely summer.

I got so that I didn't want Bob to go home, so he stayed the night. When Julie found out, she ran away, taking her sisters, Lisa and Adele with her. She went to Tadcaster, to her nannan's. I was devastated. My mum should have sent them all home in a taxi, but no, she kept Julie. I had to go to court and the judge said, 'The young ones are to be returned to their mother, but Julie is 16 years of age, my hands are tied.'

Chapter 4

I suppose that she was a very mixed up young lady at that time. She went to live with her father for a few weeks, but wasn't happy there. His girlfriend spoke unkindly of her, so she went back to her nannan's at Tadcaster.

I used to meet her every Saturday, outside Mark's and Spencer's in York, and begged her to come home. Unfortunately, she wouldn't. She had started Technical College, doing a cookery course, but packed it in. She didn't know what she wanted, poor kid. I cried every day for her to return.

I still loved Bob and drew comfort from him, but when he wanted me to set a date to marry I said no, thinking, 'What next will go wrong with us all living together?' I wanted to leave it for a few years. Bob said, 'That's no good for me.' He left saying, 'If you change your mind, you go and book the wedding.' I thought, 'Not me!'

We were very busy on the wards at work and I was glad to get home and flop into the chair with a coffee and a cigarette. Then, all at once, he appeared... JESUS!

I knew it was Jesus. Don't ask me how I knew, I just did. He was laid on his side, with his arm stretched out toward me. He spoke, 'Help me, help me. Please help me.'

I stood up and walked towards him, still holding my cigarette and coffee. 'Help you?' I can't help you! How can I help you?' I asked. He disappeared and I knew what he wanted me to do... to marry Bob. So, I went and booked the wedding for

May, when sister let me have time off. Bob was so pleased, and so were the kids.

Chapter 5

My ward sister wasn't sure that I was doing the right thing. She said it was too quick after only eleven months. I was very sure now and we bought my wedding dress from Hull. It was a long cream and blue size 12. I was very slim in those days. Bob bought a grey suit and looked very smart. We had a lovely wedding. There were only seventeen of us. Mum and Dad and Julie came at the last minute. I was so pleased to see them. It made my day. We ended up making friends. Bob's brother, Alan, and his wife and children came along with their five children.

I had a lovely cake and my dad got his wallet out and paid for the lot, bless his heart.

I was back at work on Monday and just as busy and just as glad to get home... this time Bob's home, a lovely modern centrally heated house. I made myself a coffee and lit a cigarette and went into the lounge, and there was Jesus. He was smiling. His face was radiant. He was so happy and smiling away. I knew I had done what he wanted me to do. He never spoke; just had a wonderful sunshine smile, then disappeared. I have never seen him since. I know that he is watching over our family. We have had so many miracles. Julie came home on the Wednesday.

Chapter 6

The years that followed were very busy, with hardly time to think. Julie got a job in an office, she was quite clever. She did the wages.

Bob and I were both working and the children were at school, with evening clubs, Girl Guides then the Girls' Nautical Training Corps. We were very proud of them in this organisation; they looked so smart. They were also quite musical and were in the band. They played in Homestead Park in York and at Osbaldwick. Mum and Dad came to see them. We went to see them in a drill competition at Hull and it was very impressive. Lisa excelled at running; she could run like the wind.

We were two families in one. It worked out quite well. It wasn't easy but Bob said to me, 'Stick together with me Jo, shoulder to shoulder, and don't let the daylight through where the children are concerned.' It worked well. Bob was firm but fair and it paid off.

As the children grew we were over-crowded so we built two double bedrooms, with a shower room.

The girls were happy together. They made a dance up to John Travolta music. It was great to watch them. What a laugh they had rehearsing it! Jenny still does it as her party piece with her husband. She did it recently at her 40th birthday party in Germany, where her husband was stationed.

Chapter 7

I have just remembered the lovely holiday at Newquay in about 1978, in a posh hotel. I don't know how we could have afforded it, as there were six of us. Julie was working and didn't want to come.

The weather was perfect. The days on the beach and in the warm sea were great. Andrew got a surf board and had a whale of a time. The girls had fun with a rubber dinghy, and even went swimming at midnight in the hotel pool. It was nice being waited on at meal times. I looked round the family, their faces flushed and sunburnt, giggling because Andrew had fallen asleep in the shower.

Later, he went as a punk rocker in the fancy dress competition. He was only about 10 years old. 'It was the best holiday I have ever had!', he said. We all agreed.

Back home and the girls needed pocket money. We couldn't afford it, so they all got Saturday jobs. They already had morning paper rounds. They were all good workers, except Andrew, who tried to get out of everything and got teased for it from the girls. It wasn't easy being the only boy with four sisters.

Chapter 8

Came their work years and they all got good jobs; Jenny in the Yorkshire Penny Bank, Andrew at Ben Johnson with his dad, Lisa at Lloyds Bank and Adele at York City Treasury.

Then, the birds started to fly the nest, one by one, into the world. First, into flats, then, over the years, we had four beautiful weddings.

So, the house was empty now; just Bob and I... then disaster struck. I injured my spine at work, lifting a nineteen stone stroke patient. They wheeled me off the ward in a wheelchair. It was such a bad injury that I was unable to work again.

I had to sign a form to say that I would never try to apply for work with the hospital again and they would give me a small pension.

It was like a bad dream. I couldn't take it at first. I thought I would get better in time but I never did. I couldn't do any type of job or vacuum, or carry heavy shopping or walk up hills and steps. I was in great pain for years.

I had the nerves severed in my spine, supposedly to give me a higher pain level. This was not a success and so they gave me a T.E.N.S machine; a device that scrambles the pain message going to the brain. This helped a lot, and as the pain was deadened, made the pain more bearable. Thank God.

Chapter 9

I met some ladies in the pub; Mary, Rita and another lady. Nice ladies, all divorced. Bob was working all hours, bless him. So, I was glad of the company.

We went into York and as we came out of a pub, we saw an old Mission Hall on Swinegate. Rita said, 'I used to go there as a kid, let's go in as I can hear them singing.' We all trouped in, laughing. The doorman was very nice and let us sit on the back row. The singing was beautiful. The girls were touched and so was I. They sang a song, 'Reign in Me, Sovereign Lord, Reign in Me'. I remembered it from school.

The preacher had been pulling at our heartstrings with his preaching and then this song. It was all too much to bear and I cried. They were still singing and the Pastor said, 'If you want to make it your prayer and ask Jesus into your heart, then now is the time.'

The people were raising their hands in worship. So did I, and I asked Jesus to reign in me. Well, it was like fire had hit me down my raised arm and into my chest... Wham! It was beautiful fire. Jesus had come into my heart because I had asked him to.

After that experience, I started going to that church regularly. The people were warm and friendly. I had never heard anything like the preaching before. I felt as though I had just started to live again. It was very exciting. I got baptised and I was happy.

Chapter 10

I made a nice Christian friend, called Kath Green. We went to an art class together for a time. Art was the only thing I could do because I was disabled. (I hate saying that word). Anyway, my sister-in-law, Hilary, got me interested in art. She gave me some paints for china painting. Good old Hilary. It opened up a whole new lifestyle. Years later, after many art lessons, I started my own art group. The art teacher had died and we ladies decided to carry on the class on our own. I ran the art class for seven years.

I went to Christian coffee mornings and enjoyed the company. They all had great faith in Jesus and that he still does miracles today.

Some time later, I became very ill with a thyroid problem and a lump in my neck. I had tests at the hospital, which confirmed it was the thyroid.

I was poorly, but I went to one of the coffee mornings where a black preacher form Africa was going; a mighty man of God, so they said, and he sure was. He prayed for me. He said the lump in my neck would be gone with the week, and all would be well.

The days passed by, then one morning, it happened, just as he had said. The lump disappeared! I felt completely well again. At my next hospital appointment the doctor couldn't believe it. He did another blood test, and it was negative. Hallelujah!

I told the doctor about the black preacher praying for me and that Jesus still heals today. He laughed at me, unbelievably.

It took four more visits to the hospital over the months, with four more blood tests proving negative before he was convinced. On my last visit, he said that all the tests had proved negative and asked, 'Could you get that Jesus chap to come to my clinic and get my numbers down?' I laughed and walked out of the hospital, feeling on top of the world and thanking God for healing me.

Me and Bob 1978

On our wedding Day

On holiday with the children at Uncle Fred's at Somerset

Bob enjoying the cricket

Courting with the kids in tow

Me and Bob at Scarborough

Grandad and April Louise Little poppet

Jenny and Dad

Lisa's first wedding

Ziggy Levi Dudman (our Andrew's lad)

Our grandchildren, bar 1, together to celebrate my 70th

Adam at his graduation

Our 'little' Lisa in the Sea Cadets

26

One of our traditional Dudman Boxing Day family get togethers (great memories of the kid's plays!)

Heather with our great granddaughter, baby Avah Louise

Grandson Nathan and baby daughter

Julie and her nephew and nieces loving a story time together

Me with my grandkids

Julie and Adele and all their children

Bob was a big union man for the printing factory. Here he was receiving an award for long service

Chapter 11

In the years that followed, the grandchildren started arriving. My daughter Adele, was the first to conceive. She was over the moon and so excited. she burst into our house laughing and crying at the same time with her news. She called her baby son Nathan James Robert; a lovely little baby but with awful colic. We used to sit him in our kitchen sink in warm soapy water, to sooth his tummy. I prayed for Nathan when he had been like it for a couple of months. It stopped, thank the Lord.

The next to be born was Rebecca, born to Lisa and Steve, in Pontefract. Lisa had a terrible pregnancy. She was so sick that she had to be admitted to Pontefract Hospital, where she suffered for weeks with constant sickness. She was very dehydrated and was put on a drip. She was so ill that we thought we may lose her. Adele and I went through most days, even in the snow. Julie and Bob came when they could. Julie spoke to the ward sister about Lisa. Wasn't there anything else they could do? Lisa had turned yellow and she couldn't even keep water down.

She was very weak, poor darling. The sister said they had done all they could. We all felt so helpless but then, I remembered, Jesus heals today!

I went to church and asked them all to pray for Lisa. Adele went to Pontefract alone to sit with Lisa. She said that a wonderful thing happened. It must have been about the time we were praying for Lisa at church in Haxby. Lisa suddenly swung her legs out of bed and said they were tingling. She drank a glass of water, and got out of bed, even though she had been too weak to walk. She got hold of her drip stand and walked to the day room and watched football. Adele was amazed and delighted and so were the hospital staff. From that day onward, Lisa got better.

Lisa's doctor was from Africa and had knowledge of malnutrition and put Lisa on some marvellous tablets to build up the strength she had lost through her sickness. The people at church praised God for answered prayer. God is good.

When Lisa gave birth, her baby, Rebecca was fine, although Grandad said she looked as if she had been in a boxing match! Her little eyes and lips were so swollen. Rebecca grew into a beautiful little child.

Adam was next to be born to my eldest daughter, Julie. her husband, John, was quite rude and outspoken to me on our first meeting. This was really upsetting, as you want everything to go well in families.

The following day was a Sunday and on my way to church I was grumbling to myself about how rude John was to me. Suddenly a voice said, 'Thank you God for John.' It was an audible voice, and although it came out of my mouth, it was not me speaking. I spun around, there was no-one else in the street. I was quite alone, or was I?

Chapter 12

It was the Lord who spoke through me. It was the most amazing experience. Since then, I have thanked God for John; nearly every day. He has turned out to be a lovely dad to both their children. They had a little girl next, called Laura. I loved her as soon as I saw her.

Adele gave birth to April; such a treasure. When she was about two years old she climbed up onto the chair and picked up a red hot iron. Her mummy had been ironing jeans, so it was very hot. Little April held the hot iron to her bare chest. I couldn't believe what I was seeing. Adele screamed. I kept calm and held my hand out for the iron. April smiled sweetly at me and handed me the iron. There wasn't a mark on her. How wonderful of the Lord. He protected April. He must have put his hand on her little chest. Adele seemed in shock, she could barely believe what she had just witnessed. April was such a poppet. I was able to tell her about Jesus and also her little sister, Paige. As they grew, I took them both to Sunday School for a while, and they asked Jesus into their hearts; so did Rebecca and her little brother Luke. They were happy days, when my grandchildren were little. Now they are grown up and Rebecca is starting work after the Christmas holidays. She will be teaching PE in schools.

Chapter 13

One summer's day, it was about 1996, our Jenny came to visit with a friend from work. She was now nursing, so was observant and noticed that I was in pain. I admitted I was and I was under the hospital waiting to see Mr. Bogdon, because I had very painful lumps in my breasts.

At the time, the hospital waiting lists were very long and I had been waiting a considerable length of time.

Jenny got onto the phone to the hospital and tried her very best to plead my case, as I was in pain, but to no avail.

That night, my dear friend, Kath Green, came round with an audio tape for me to listen to about God's healing power. She left it with me and I listened to it alone.

At first, I just smiled because the American lady preached sounded like Yogi Bear. As I got used to the accent I heard her say. 'God split the Red Sea, so he can heal your body!' I thought, 'That's true!', and I asked Jesus to heal me. Nothing happened. But, by the next morning, when I woke, I was completely healed. The lumps had gone. Fantastic!

My husband was amazed. 'You are alright, aren't you, gal.' He said. 'Yes, yes, Jesus has healed me.' I cried. 'It's wonderful, no pain, no lumps, they are completely gone!' I was besides myself with happiness. I could go back to my ordinary bra now. I had been wearing big awful comfy ones.

I made an appointment with my family doctor. He was very surprised but told me to attend the hospital appointment with it finally came up. I kept the appointment with Mr. Bogdon, who examined me and then got a second opinion. He then wrote, in a large ledger book. 'This patient was healed due to a religious experience.' I went home singing. 'Wow, what a mighty God! Thank you, Jesus.' I was on cloud nine. I wanted to tell the world.

Chapter 14

One day, as I was waiting for the Reliance bus, a very strange thing happened. I was chatting to a very nice lady. She had rosy cheeks and black hair. She told me about a strange dream that she had the night before, and wondered if it had a meaning. She dreamed that she was baking and into her bowl of white flour lots of tiny black flies appeared and spoilt the flour. That's all she said.

Just then, the bus came and we got on. I was alone and asked the Lord, 'What does that dream mean, Lord Jesus?'

Straight away, he told me. The flour is her life and the black flies are the things that are spoiling her life. 'Wow!', I said. When we got to town I walked alongside her. I told her I was a Christian and that I had asked Jesus what her dream meant, and he told me. She looked surprised, but was curious, so I told her. But, I said, 'Only you know the thing that you have to get rid of.'

'Yes, thank you', she said, and hurried off.

Chapter 15

It was about seven years later that I was reading my Bible and I saw her face. It just appeared and every time I opened my Bible, there she was again. I asked one of my church leaders what to do. He prayed with me and asked the Lord to guide me to her, as she may need help, in some way.

Well, I was very nervous. I didn't know where she lived or even her name. I set off the next day, to find her. I tried the bungalows near the Reliance bus stop. I knocked at a door, it opened, but it wasn't her. I told the lady that I was looking for someone and described her. I said she used to get the Reliance bus into York. 'Oh, that's my next door neighbour', she exclaimed. 'She is out now, but I will tell her you called. She visits her husband who is in hospital, every day. Come back tomorrow morning and you will catch her in.'

The next day, I nervously went and knocked at the neighbour's door. The lady I had met seven years earlier was no more. Her black hair was grey and her rosy cheeks had gone. Her face was pale and drawn. She recognised me and asked me into the kitchen. I blurted out something about seeing her face every time I opened my Bible. she nodded. She looked worn out.

Chapter 16

The lady had been having a very stressful time of it. Backwards and forwards to the hospital, to see her husband, every day. She said she had seen a vision of the Christ child at the head of her bed. I asked her if she had ever given her life to Jesus. She said, 'No.'

I gave her a holy picture of Jesus, standing at a door, knocking. I said, 'Jesus stands at the door of our hearts and knocks and waits for us to ask him into our lives. I asked her if she would like to do that, because Jesus said, 'come unto me all you who are heavy laden and troubled and I will give you rest.' (Matthew 11:28)

She cried and joined me in the prayer of salvation, asking Jesus into her heart and life. What a transformation. The roses came back into her cheeks, she was laughing and crying and said, 'I feel like a load has been lifted from me.' She hugged me and asked my name and told me hers.

As I left, I felt I was walking on air. 'Thank you Jesus', I said aloud. 'Bless you and hooray!'. The next day I returned and left her a Bible on her doorstep. God is good!

Chapter 17

(I was feeling much better today, so I went to ASDA with Bob. I had really bad chest pains (when I was near the toilet rolls) and ended up having an ECG at the doctors. I was clear, thank the Lord.

I feel really wiped out, so I have settled down in my big arm chair to write again.)

Some years ago, my brother, John, phoned me and asked me to go and see his life long friend, Susan, in ICU, at the District hospital. She was on a life support machine and was getting weaker. First, I wrote to Susan and Lennie, her husband. I told them I was a Christian now and believed in Jesus and that he still heals today. I told them about the power of the Holy Spirit coming into your life when you ask Jesus into your heart. Well, they both believed this and said a prayer of salvation.

So, when I arrived there, the three of us came into agreement for Susan's healing. 'In Jesus' name and by his wounds you are healed', I said.

I quickly left because I was nervous and a bit shy, anyway my brother phoned me three days later and said Susan was going home as she was well!!

So thank you Jesus praise God. God is so good!

Chapter 18

Our little Lisa sadly got divorced. She got a tiny house with her two children, Rebecca and Luke. Grandad helped her decorate. Lisa is very good at interior design. It looked very nice. Then Lisa met a nice chap at work, and fell in love. A year later, they were married. It was a beautiful wedding and her nieces and daughter were bridesmaids. Her son Luke, and nephews, Adam and Nathan, together with Duncan (Shaun's nephew) were ushers.

It was a very grand do. The weather was really hot and we all spilled out onto the lawns for photos, in the sunshine. Our Jenny came over from Germany for the wedding with her three boys. Jenny's husband is in the RAF and was away on business so he was unable to come. Lisa and her husband, Shaun, and children moved into a lovely four bedroomed house with a big garden.

Shaun wanted family, but Lisa had stopped ovulating and could not conceive. She was devastated. Adele was so sorry for her sister that she offered to be a surrogate mother for her. I thought it better to pray for Lisa first. I anointed Lisa with oil, with a little sign of the cross on her forehead.

She was crying and very distraught. I asked Jesus to bless Lisa with a baby. Well, God is good and Lisa conceived, although she had another very difficult pregnancy and ended up in hospital again, on a drip, because of her constant sickness.

Chapter 19

Lisa was so sick again that she couldn't keep even sips of water sown, so I asked my Christian friends for prayer for Lisa and the baby.

One of my friends, Ken, prophesied that both mother and baby daughter would be okay and said that, 'The baby girl will grow up to be used of the Lord, and you will live to see this.'

Well, all is well and the baby is now two years old. She is called Daisy, and is the apple of her father's eye.

Some time ago I felt the Lord telling me to read my Bible more, so I joined a Bible study group. There is so much to learn. I was involved in 'Women Aglow', an international Christian woman's society. I took my two friends, Christine and Cynthia. Christine went forward for prayer one evening and asked Jesus into her heart. Bless God.

One day my son-in-law, Barry, phoned and told me that Adele had an auto immune syndrome and the hospital had given her only five years to live. 'Dear God,' I said, 'Why didn't you tell me before Barry?' She had kept if from me for two years. Now she was very poorly. The ladies from Woman Aglow were all praying for Adele. I took her in my arms and asked Jesus to heal her. 'By your wounds we are healed, in Jesus name', I said loud and clear. The Lord is good and merciful. Adele had an overnight miracle. The next day, she was at her sister's, jumping on a trampoline. What a mighty God he is! Thank you Jesus.

Chapter 20

I went to see an old friend, Jennifer. She was very depressed and had been like that for years. I asked her if I could pray with her and she agreed. 'I bind depression in you in Jesus name', I said. I asked her to ask Jesus into her life and she did. Praise the Lord. Her depression left her and she has never felt like that again. God is good.

Chapter 21

This last story is about Stella, another dear old friend who I met in town, and who I led to the Lord a couple of years ago. She was grieving over the death of her sister.

Recently, Stella's daughter, Anna, phoned me and asked me to visit her mum, on the ICU as she was dying. I went and Stella was in a coma. I spoke to her but the ward sister said, 'She won't hear you.' I thought to myself, her spirit will. I reminded her spirit how she became born again a couple of years ago. I quoted the Bible, again Isaiah 53:5, 'By his wounds we are healed.' I then came away as it was so sad to see her like that. She had a clot on her brain, pushing her eye out. She was stone deaf in one ear because of the diseased eardrum and many more things wrong.
'We are keeping her comfortable', the sister said.

Her family were waiting to see her so I went home. Later, Anna phoned and said her mum raised both arms in the air and opened one eye when I left. Thank you Jesus.

Chapter 22

Anna was overjoyed at the instant improvement of her mum. She rang me and said, 'It's you that's done it.' I said, 'Anna, I couldn't heal a fly. Its Jesus and his words in the Bible that has done it,' I insisted.

The following day, I went back and took biscuits for the staff, as they were so kind to Stella. Well, I was pleased to see that she was propped up in bed and talking, as well as she could (with a tube in her mouth). I took her a Bible and she was pleased to see me and patted my hand.

Her husband asked her to marry him all over again. She said, 'Yes.' I left there praising God.

I didn't go again for over a week but I phoned Anna who said her mum was okay but stone deaf. I put her on the Woman Aglow prayer chain. They said, 'Please let Stella's ear pop open, we ask this in Jesus name.'

I went to see Stella the next day. She had been transferred to a ward days before. Stella greeted me with joy, and said, 'My ear is fine. Yesterday it popped open and I can hear again,' she said, 'and I am going home tonight.'

Life is very exciting working for Jesus. He is the way, the truth and the life. His word is truth. No-one comes to the Father except through Jesus. He loves every one of us. The good, the bad and the ugly.

He wants to have a personal relationship with us. You don't have to be 'good enough', just as you are, warts and all.

Ask him into your life today. You will never regret it. Go for it. God is good.

Joan's Story

2020

To wake up to the realisation that you are 80 years old, its so incredible and hard to believe in one's head!

My eldest daughter, Julie, prepared a family gathering for my 80th birthday party, bless her. She is so good to me. There were about 40 people invited and only a couple declined. Tom, who although coming up from Oxford University, caught Mumps! Poor lad! So, he spent some time with his other grandma and could not come to my party.

The party was a great success. All my lovely grandchildren and great grandchildren and the mums and dads all turned up with gifts and good wishes and it was just wonderful. Grandad paid for a meal for everyone; a roast dinner at Toby Carvery.

Our Julie and Jenny went ahead and prepared the private room and decorated it with Happy Birthdays and an 80th balloon. My granddaughter Paige, made the most beautiful cake, shaped in a big heart; showing my big heart for all the family!

Bobby and I were overwhelmed that so many people went out of their way to come and see us. Luke came from London, all that way, bless him, up to York. Becky came from Sheffield, heavily pregnant with twin girls. She came with her lovely partner, Jon. Jenny came from Ripon, with her husband Mewsie. My brother and his wife came from Boston Spa. It was especially difficult for John's wife, Jane, because she was lame and due for a hip replacement, but she came, bless her. My nephew, Peter, came from Leeds with his lovely family. it was wonderful to see everybody. We were bowled over with Joy!!!

My 80th Birthday party with all my precious family

The icing on the cake – my beautiful 80th Birthday cake!

My friends at church made a fuss of me the next day. There were four of us with Birthdays and we all had a lovely time and Dorothy put a beautiful spread on for us! She is a wonderful lady and makes us all welcome at church, and in her home.

My friend Andy, from Roko, came to see me a few days before, with a pot full of beautiful flowers. The Lord had really blessed Andy about a year ago. She came into Roko assisted by her husband, as she could hardly walk, and was bent double with a type of arthritis. She said she had to be dressed and assisted in all ways. He husband assisted her into the pool. It looked very painful for her to climb down the wall bars.

When she had been in the pool for a little while, I swam over to her and she told me what was wrong. At hospital the doctors had given up on her, as she wouldn't take their medication, which was not doing her any good at all.

I asked her if she would like me to pray for her healing. She said she did not believe in God, but that it would be okay for me to pray. So, I went ahead and prayed for healing in Jesus name. I swam off hoping for the best, and although I believe and have received miracles myself, what happened was absolutely amazing. About a week later I saw Andy again and she walked into the swimming pool area with her back straight and limbs supple and smiling, and said she was absolutely fine! Thank you Jesus! Thank you Jesus! She never looked back and she is absolutely healed from the top of her head to the tips of her toes, just like I had asked Jesus to heal her! Our God is faithful and so, so good!

I am meeting Andy for coffee this morning. We have stayed friends for over a year now. I am still amazed at such a wonderful healing! God is so good. But, Andy still does not believe in God! That is so sad. But, thank you Jesus for your wonderful miracles in our lives. You love us so much, you are absolutely wonderful to us.

One fine day, people may wake up to the realisation of your love and power! Only you can save us from eternal life without you, a life of darkness and despair eternally! People only have to believe in you to have eternal life of love and peace and joy! I know which I choose...

I choose you, Lord!

Printed in Great Britain
by Amazon